LIVING

IN A VOID

*How the Coronavirus
Pandemic affected our Lives*

IBRAHIM OLAWALE

First published in Great Britain as a softback original in 2021

Copyright © Ibrahim Olawale

The moral right of this author has been asserted.

All rights reserved.

No part of this publication may be reproduced, stored in a retrieval system, or transmitted, in any form or by any means, without the prior permission in writing of the author, nor be otherwise circulated in any form of binding or cover other than that in which it is published and without a similar condition including this condition being imposed on the subsequent purchaser.

Design by Buzzdesignz

Published by The Roaring Lion Newcastle LTD.

ISBN: 978-1-913636-86-9

Email: books@theroaringlionnewcastle.com

Website:
www.theroaringlionnewcastle.com

DEDICATION

This book is dedicated to humanity for standing strong and in alliance to fight against the deadly virus, to all the scientists and health care frontline workers who risked it all to save and protect humanity from the deadly virus and to every family that has encountered loss(es) during these trying times.

TABLE OF CONTENTS

Acknowledgements 1

Chapter One: The Outbreak 2

Chapter Two: Living In A Void 12

Chapter Three: Family Under Lockdown 24

Chapter Four: Love Under Lockdown 43

Chapter Five: The Pandemic And The Economy 62

Chapter Six: The New Normal 76

Bio 88

Author's Note 89

ACKNOWLEDGEMENTS

With love in my heart, I am grateful to everyone who has contributed immensely to the success of this book. The world is a safer place thanks to people who have dedicated their lives to uphold the human race despite our continuous challenges.

To my ever-supportive mum, my powerful role model who taught me love and kindness; and to my friends and family (without their support and experience, this book would be non-existent), thank you.

Chapter One

THE OUTBREAK

"The outbreak of COVID-19 has created an unprecedented situation around the world."
*- **Ram Nath Kovind***

The year 2020 began with harrowing news for everyone. The world was on fire—literally. A new virus appeared on the block, the coronavirus (COVID-19). The world shut down, countries went on lockdown, cities and towns were placed on quarantine, health facilities became overwhelmed, and economic and social activities took back stage in the face of survival.

Countries closed their borders against travel, people were forced to stay in their houses for months, and stringent measures, including the regular washing of hands, social distancing, the use of face masks, use of alcohol-based sanitizers, and other safety measures, were advocated by governments and those responsible for responding to and battling against the virus.

The whole world was brought to its knees.

Human emotions around this time were marked with fear, uncertainty, and tension, as millions of people were turning up sick all over the world and thousands were dying. Humanity faced its greatest challenge in a long time—one not limited to a certain region, race, or location—and it seemed like the end of the world was in sight with the advent of the coronavirus and its global influence, compared to previous deadly pandemics like the bubonic plague and influenza (which ravaged only Europe) or Ebola (which emerged only in a few regions and took tens of millions of lives).

The coronavirus was first discovered at a seafood and animal market in Wuhan, China, in December 2019, when what seemed like an outbreak of pneumonia broke out amongst its populace without an obvious underlying cause. Before the city of Wuhan was put on lockdown, several people had moved out of the city to other destinations, unknowingly spreading the virus in what became the fastest and widest spread of a virus in the history of humankind, due to its far-reaching global impact.

The whole world paused for days, weeks, and then months as both governments and health experts alike tried to identify the virus amidst the growing number of cases, how it worked, how it could be contracted, if the virus could be contained, and its probable impact on the economy and the lives of their citizens.

Amidst the rise of the virus, there were growing opinions that this was an act of the Chinese government to cripple the world economy in their favour—a malicious attempt to wrest world power from the United States of America and other power blocs. This seemed especially so with the way China effectively set up state of the art health facilities in less than a week of the pandemic to mitigate the virus; the fact that, at the time, the whole world was suffering from the impact of the virus; that it never went beyond two cities in China; the controversy surrounding the lab in which the virus was said to have broken out in Wuhan; and the subsequent deaths of those lab workers who had allegedly expressed concerns before the outbreak.

The then-United States President Donald Trump sparked and continued to fan the flames of this conspiracy theory as he kept emphasizing that the virus was the *Chinese Virus,* saying "It came from China, hence it is the Chinese virus." That statement alone, repeated often by President Donald Trump, and the fact that China was not forthcoming in divulging the circumstances concerning the outbreak said a lot, at the time.

The coronavirus disease (COVID-19) is caused by a novel strain of coronavirus, Severe Acute Respiratory Syndrome Coronavirus 2 (SARS-CoV-2). It is part of a group of viruses that can cause respiratory and gastrointestinal diseases in humans. Scientist and health experts believe that the new strain of coronavirus (SARS-CoV-2) likely originated in bats or pangolins as another variation of the vast family of coronaviruses present in animals like camels, bats, raccoon, dogs, cats, and others; seven of which are known to cause disease in humans.

Starting from the period the virus was first discovered in December 2019 to the time the World Health Organization declared COVID-19 a global pandemic in March 2020, there were already confirmed cases of 509,164 infected people and 23,335 deaths globally (according to the World Health Organization's statistics), and the numbers which were steadily rising by the day would later run into millions for both categories.

Symptoms of COVID-19 included fever, dry cough, difficulty breathing, tiredness, aches and pains, sore throat, diarrhea, conjunctivitis, headache, loss of taste or smell, a rash on the skin, or discoloration of the fingers or toes. More than half of all cases of COVID-19 remained asymptomatic, making it hard to determine who really had the virus, without proper testing.

The virus is transferable through contact with respiratory droplets carrying infectious virus, which is then transferred to another person through the eyes, nose, or mouth. Coughing, sneezing, talking, and touching are the means of transmission, and it can be transferred through airborne transmission of droplets for around six feet—hence the need for social distancing. Further testing also led to the discovery that droplets could linger on hard surfaces for up to 72 hours, and that touching a surface where infected droplets lingered and then touching the mouth, nose, or eyes could also transfer the virus.

Several groups of people were found to be more at risk of having severe cases of COVID-19 (mostly older people with underlying health issues), and around 13 percent of people over the age of 75 who have the disease and fall sick will die.

The CDC published a summary of conditions that come with the significant risk of severe COVID-19 illness. They include those who have asthma, hypertension, immune deficiencies, liver disease, cancer, cerebrovascular disease, chronic kidney disease, COPD (chronic obstructive pulmonary disease), diabetes mellitus, heart conditions, and other diseases.

The outbreak of coronavirus came in three waves. The first wave was from January 23 through March 21, 2020, representing the inception of the virus as it spread steadily from China to other countries of the world. Lockdowns and quarantines were effective, and were enforced by most governments.

The second wave was from March through July 4, 2020, exacerbated, especially, because of the easing up of lockdown in some countries from May to April, which made the number of cases and deaths increase drastically to over 500,000.

This was seen in Italy, the United States, and several other European countries, at the time. The governments of these affected countries were forced to reinstate lockdown protocols, and other countries enforced strict screening procedures for travellers from these places.

The third wave was from July 5 through December 2, 2020, wherein Hong Kong was hit hard, as well as Maharashtra, India, with 66,159 fresh cases and 771 fatalities within a short period of time. These steadily increased through the whole of India.

Due to the virus that was COVID-19, powerful, high-income countries with ultra-modern healthcare systems quickly found themselves incapacitated, with official reports declaring the largest numbers of confirmed cases to be in the United States, Italy, Spain, and France; with the United States, India, and Brazil experiencing the highest mortality.

In the words of the Italian Prime Minister Giuseppe Conte, "Our hospitals, despite their efficiency, risk being overwhelmed. We have a problem with intensive care units." His fears turned out to be real, as Italy and a few other European countries with seemingly great healthcare systems soon became overwhelmed in the first few months of the virus outbreak.

As the virus developed and surfaced in various countries of the world, another issue of global concern became the fear that, amongst third world countries, Africa would have the highest fatality rates in the face of the challenges posed by COVID-19.

American philanthropist Melinda Gates, in the early days of the virus, expressed that she feared Africa would be unable to deal with the problem of COVID-19, and that it would get to such a peak that there would be bodies lying on the streets. Another report released by the United Nations Economic Commission for Africa (UNECA) stated in April that "Anywhere between 300,000 to 3.3 million Africans could lose their lives due to COVID-19."

Contrary to all opinions, these fears for Africa turned out to be unfounded. After the first case of COVID-19 was reported in Africa (from Egypt, on February 14 2020), the African Union Commission (AU) convened for an emergency meeting of all ministers of health through the African Centre for Disease Control and Prevention (Africa CDC). They succeeded in drafting strategies to battle the virus throughout the African continent, including targeting surveillance and testing, providing medical supplies, addressing public health and social measures, putting into place preventive practices, and providing welfare.

We saw many African countries bring to the foregound their long experiences in dealing with infectious diseases, with countries like Uganda, Senegal, Rwanda, and others redirecting their screening and containment efforts from combating Ebola to deal with COVID-19 even before it got to their borders.

The full understanding of these African governments about their inadequacies when it came to healthcare also helped to enforce these prevention measures, unlike their Western counterparts, who were hit harder.

The low number of cases and deaths in Africa (which didn't number 150,000 in the whole continent at the end of year 2020) brought about the first hypothesis that the geography and climate had something to do with the low impact of the virus, but this line of thought was later dropped after testing by scientists proved it to be untrue.

Apart from African countries, countries like Taiwan, New Zealand, Iceland, Singapore, and Vietnam also set up quick responses, mitigating the number of deaths in their countries to lower than a hundred deaths, to date.

After the initial fears and worries about the virus came science's pursuit of a cure—a task that proved to be daunting and almost impossible in the face of the uniqueness of the virus.

Maria Van Kerkhove, an epidemiologist with the World Health Organization, says, simply, "We are humbled by this virus." Such was the case of scientists of the world as they raced against time for a cure and made little or no headway in the initial stages.

It was first believed that chloroquine could serve as a cure for coronavirus, a belief that had lots of countries and medical establishments hoarding and exploring that path; but this turned out to be untrue for almost 97 percent of cases. The coronavirus seemed to have come to stay.

People were dying in thousands, and those at home were getting tired of the lockdown and the inactivity that came with it. It seemed as if the only way to battle the virus was for humanity to separate itself as best as it could, sequestering in the safe confines of houses until those with the virus were totally healed and the virus gone.

In the words of Donald Trump in a speech at the White House, made on February 17 2020, "It's going to disappear. One day, it's like a miracle; it will disappear." But, that was not to be. That expectation of his that the virus would go out of existence just like it came, coupled with slow response reactions, spelled problems for the United States, as they were hit hard by the pandemic.

It wasn't until November through December of 2020 that scientists finally made a breakthrough on the COVID-19 vaccine after much testing, and this was finally made public around the same time.

Along with the arrival of the vaccines came a new challenge that cropped up: the inability to produce the vaccine in the large quantities needed to vaccinate the whole world and everyone who needed it, as numbers continued to rise in several places like Hong Kong and India.

Dr. Michael Osterholm, Director of the Center for Infectious Disease Research and Policy, said, "We had many more arms that wanted vaccines than the vaccine was available. Now, it's no longer the last mile. It is solely down to the last inch, getting the needles in people's arms."

In the light of the COVID-19 pandemic, one thing we saw was how close-knit the world was. The fact that a virus that began in Wuhan, China, could spread to the whole world in a matter of weeks and hold everyone ransom pointed to the increased level of globalization and integration across international borders, and its latent opportunities and disadvantages. The ability of a health issue in a small part of the world to spread to the whole world showed how the world was being slowly de-territorialised.

Sociologically, the pandemic disrupted social relations and the feeling of interconnectedness amongst people, especially with the enforcement of social/physical distancing and quarantines and lockdowns which negated social interaction, the foundation of human existence.

In the face of the fear, tension, having to remain alone, and everything that came with the coronavirus and lockdowns, people began questioning their ideals of physical and social interactions, disconnecting themselves from society in what is gradually becoming the new normal.

Chapter Two

LIVING IN A VOID

"If you look long enough into the void, the void begins to look back through you." —***Friedrich Nietzsche***

Relationships and interactions with others are what make life interesting—the myriad emotions that come with being in the company of family, friends, work colleagues and acquaintances. At the epicenter of humankind's search for happiness, fulfillment, and relaxation are physical and social interaction as a means of satisfying these cravings.

We party with friends, go sightseeing, hang out with loved ones, watch movies at the cinema, immerse ourselves in nature, take walks, or simply sit in the park and watch others go about their lives as a way of finding and adding meaning into our lives.

There is also that burning need of man to be engaged; the inherent need to always be in motion as we dream those big dreams, pursue our goals, rush towards our jobs for that promotion or to get that next paycheck that would solve some of those *needs* and *wants* we believe would make our lives better, and desire to just not be idle. Humans have always had plans or goals governing every stage of our existence, with our lives following a pattern we were supposed to have predetermined (or, one the system had programmed us to follow).

But, what happens when all these are taken away and relationships and interactions are abruptly paused?

Voids begin to appear!

These voids, smaller at first, begin to expand as relationships and interactions continue to be estranged and an inability to fill it with anything worthwhile begins a downward spiral towards mental and emotional crisis. In the words of author Eva Pierrakos, "Your outer willpower may also have succeeded in building an eventful outer life that fills the *void* to a degree, as long as you do not hold still. However, this is but a temporary peace before the storm."

A void is an empty space. In humans, it is characterized by feelings of numbness, a sense of nothingness, a lack of purpose, the lack of excitement, and the feeling of disconnection. It is a feeling of emptiness brought on by several reasons ranging from stress, loneliness, boredom, anxiety and depression, and other factors.

We humans are said to have six basic emotional needs: love and connection, security, significance, growth, meaning, and purpose. These emotions stem from our interactions, and also depend on these interactions to fuel them.

It is in this vein that psychologists and sociologists hold social relations to be the building blocks of a society that has evolved to give meaning to the life, aspirations, and pursuits of man. In the words of Emile Durkheim, "It is true that we take it as evidence that social life depends upon its foundation and bears its mark, just as the mental life of an individual depends upon his nervous system and in fact his whole organism. But collective consciousness is more than a mere epiphenomenon of its morphological basis, just as individual consciousness is something more than a simple efflorescence of the nervous system."

With those words, Emile Durkheim makes an emphatic statement from his years of research about human behavior, that, just as the internal organs and the neurons within the body subsist on the others to function; so do humans need to engage in interactions with others to really add meaning to their lives.

The lockdown and imposed inactivity which was a result of the COVID-19 pandemic that began in some countries in February 2020 through to the end of the year brought about a halt to humanity's frenzied race and daily pursuits. The world stood still, and the balance that humans thought to have achieved in life through social integration shredded as social interactions became banned and restrictions were placed on movement and every other facet of life in a bid to mitigate the spread of the pandemic, shaking the very core of human existence.

The isolation, compounded by mass panic and anxiety, brought about an unprecedented challenge to humankind—one we have never had to face in a very long epoch of human history—the challenge of living with one's self. Due to globalization, interconnectedness, and the interdependence of society, our lives have been so tuned to living in tandem with others and losing ourselves in activities, that staying put in an enclosed place all by ourselves (or with just a few loved ones for an extended period of time) posed a major monumental and existential crisis. It was like a car in high motion suddenly putting on the brakes without first easing down on its speed. A crash was inevitable.

Waking up each day to the cold reality of being alone, or to just seeing the same few faces every day, brought with it an intense feeling of loneliness and boredom. Millions found themselves lost and questioning their individuality and their place in society and the world at large. Efforts by many to find a bit of solace on social media only aggravated their feelings of panic, fear, and anxiety; especially with the negative news making rounds on the internet about the need to keep safe and the spiking numbers of infected cases and deaths, pushing them to subconsciously recoil even from the internet, and to view it through a guarded lens.

In the words of psychologist Martin Hagger, during the pandemic, "Researchers have noted marked increases in levels of stress, depression, anxiety, and loneliness in the overall population over the course of the pandemic. The effects of the pandemic are widespread and affect multiple populations and groups. Many are struggling to cope with the lack of social contact, particularly those who live alone. Younger populations and children may also have reduced social development due to lack of interpersonal context."

And so it was that, aside from the COVID-19 which was already claiming thousands of lives by the day, another crisis was imminent with each day the isolation dragged on.

It was a crisis of *self!*

And the aftereffects and impact of this crisis was predicted to transcend to new levels even after the isolation eases, as people tried to find their places in a society which is now further characterized with wariness, hidden/masked faces for preventive control, and social distancing.

Impacts of Boredom and Loneliness During the Pandemic

While the brain is the key organ for coordinating thoughts, movements, and feelings; the mind embodies sets of cognitive aspects such as consciousness, imagination, perception, intelligence, and judgment, as well as non-cognitive emotions and instincts. Both the brain and the mind are close to inseparable in their activities and impact on human lives. What we see, hear, smell, think of, plan, and do are processed, determined, and controlled by these two.

Long before the pandemic, neuroscientists have engaged in the study of how boredom (and, subsequently, loneliness) impacts the brain, behavior, and human health. They have developed a growing body of epidemiological works that point out that loneliness seems to prompt a chronic release of hormones that suppress healthy immune functions, increasing the likelihood of sickness and also aggravating whatever disease lies in the human body.

But, neuroscientist Kay Tye says, "Loneliness is inherently subjective. It is possible to spend the day completely isolated, in quiet contemplation, and still feel invigorated. Or, to stew in alienated mystery surrounded by a crowd, in the heart of a big city, or accompanied by close friends and family."

A typical example is American singer Justin Bieber. Long before the lockdown, Justin Bieber became public about the mental health issues he was battling. According to him, there were times when he felt suicidal because he was really lonely. Coming from someone who was always around people, fans, loved ones, and was always on the move from one music project to the other, this goes to show a lot. And this was the case with a myriad of other people, way before the lockdown.

Therefore, loneliness can be said to be different from being alone. You can be alone and not lonely, and you can be in the midst of people, like Justin Bieber was, and yet feel very lonely.

According to neuroscience, the brain and mind are configured in such a way that they need to be engaged all the time, and the isolation, coupled with inactivity and other destabilizing factors, brought with it a direct impact on the functioning of the brain and mind, creating and aggravating this feeling of emptiness. Experimental studies show that social isolation produces significant changes in brain structure and processes, building neural signatures that might hold lasting impacts.

With isolation and having to put a pause on everything that has occupied humankind's time, the first act of the mind is to retract itself as it tries to process everything ongoing from a seemingly-safe distance. As news filtered in about the negativities racking the world and the increasing lack of physical and social interaction that could dull these negatives, the search soon turned inwards, leading to an exploration of *self*.

The 'void feeling' is born as a result of this exploration of self, as the mind begins to consciously and subconsciously conceive new truths while embroiled in fear, anxiety, and worry—feelings which might be real, or not.

The impact of boredom and loneliness during the pandemic is far-reaching, and neuroscientists, psychologists, health experts, and all those concerned with human development have voiced concerns about future mental health crises. Although there is already a growing number of mental and emotional health issues, as reported by US authorities, within its borders and some other countries, the full effects would not be seen until later, as many had been sapped of their wills during isolation and were just winging it a step at a time; numb, empty, and living in a void.

There has been an increased use of substances and alcohol to dull these 'void feelings', posing more health issues for the future. According to the Centre for Disease Control and Prevention, there is a drastic increase in substance use as a way of coping with the stress and emotions related to COVID-19, and overdoses have also spiked.

Other ills in society have been brought to the forefront as human emotions become unstable and we try to find new meanings for our lives. There are increased cases of crime, racism, xenophobia, and more.

Facing the Void

"The only way to be happy, healthy, and whole is to face and deal with the voids you carry in your heart and soul. If something is missing, broken, or empty inside of you, there is no person or thing that will fill it. Only you can heal yourself and close the voids." —Stephenie Zamora

The feeling of emptiness and numbness that comes with living in a void makes it hard to want to come up with ways of dealing with it. Most times, we fill the void with other things like unhealthy eating patterns, drugs, alcohol, worry, recklessness, aggressive behaviors, more activities, and other things that we might think of. But, in the long run, this is only running away from the obvious; and no matter how much we run, we will still come back to meet the void there until the moment that it swallows us up totally.

The question of how to deal with this void that many have found themselves in, before it consumes them, is what constitutes fear, for experts; especially in the light of human connectedness and what the future portends. This is why I have outlined several ways to face and overcome the void.

1. Confess

The mind's way of trying to protect itself is to ignore the void feeling and hope that it is a phase that will pass, but this is never the case. The feeling doesn't pass; but rather, festers and grows by the day. You need to intentionality battle the void and overcome it, and confessing to yourself is the first step in the process.

You need to confess to yourself (and to people who really care about you) that you are living in a void. Sit back in your place of solitude, try to understand what it is that you are feeling, write it down (if you can), share this with others, and accept the fact that this is your current state of being.

2. From Isolation to Solitude

Although there is no difference between isolation and solitude, in that both involve being alone, solitude is usually actively sought after and comes from a place of personal yearning; while isolation is forced from the outside.

Solitude is a mental frame of mind in which being alone is used constructively for the expansion and freedom of thought, unaffected by any external factor, in a bid to birth new realities and soar beyond the ordinary. This is an opportunity to get a good grasp of yourself, evaluate your past pursuits, and then press forward for the future you desire to achieve.

"A man can be himself only as long as he is alone; and if he doesn't love solitude, he will not love freedom; for it is only when he is alone that he is really free." —Arthur Schopenhauer.

The worlds of art, music, literature, and even science are filled with examples of greatness birthed during solitude. The great inventor Albert Einstein says, "I lived in solitude in the country, and noticed how the monotony of quiet life stimulates the creative mind."

You can choose to see the period of isolation as a time to look within; to understand and engage in your hobbies to birth the greatness within you. It is a time of self-discovery and personal growth and development.

3. Use Technology to Connect With Others

In times of isolation and the loneliness that comes with it, connect with your loved ones through technology. Experts have maintained that this reduces the feeling of loneliness and worries that come from lack of physical and social interactions. You can use video phone technology to get in touch with family and friends.

4. Guard Yourself Against the Internet and Media

With the negative news flying around on the internet and in the media, it is very easy to lose one's self further into the void. It is advisable to guard yourself against these kinds of news reports. Limit what you see, hear, and subsequently allow your mind and brain to process.

5. Create a Schedule

We have been able to establish the need for the brain and the mind to be busy—especially, the need for the mind to feel that it is not idle, and the mental process that comes with the mind's being constantly engaged. In times of isolation during the void feeling (which mostly is birthed from inactivity), set a schedule for yourself.

Whether you are working from home or not, prepare for your day as you normally do. Maintain good hygiene, exercise within the confines of your home, take your bath, get dressed, and join online groups on subjects that interest you, such as reading, writing, the arts, or music.

6. Engage in Self-Care

You need to create time for self-care in the midst of the void. Take hot baths, read, write, listen to music, learn a new skill online, or learn how to cook from watching videos; all in a bid to keep yourself in a cheerful mood and not get lost in the depressing feeling of the void.

During the pandemic, when speaking about how he coped with his mental health, Justin Bieber said, "I pray and meditate—things like that. I write music and listen to music. Music is very powerful; it can really help you when you're feeling low."

7. Ask for Help

As much as you have come to understand and face the fact that you are living in a void, it is not always certain that anyone can overcome it all by themselves, no matter how hard they try. This can, in turn, lead to more complications. When you keep trying, yet can't seem to overcome this hurdle, the feeling of living in a void might become compounded by the frustration felt from your inability to make any headway.

Technology has made it easier to contact mental health professionals online, and to book appointments and hold sessions through Zoom meetings and other technological means. Mental health professionals will help you through the process of finding answers to the questions bothering you, and will help you facilitate the exploration and discovery of self.

You can also search for support groups to connect and relate with—people like you who are experiencing similar problems—and this will go a long way in helping you overcome the problem of the void.

***

The state of living in a void is one that comes with lots of negative implications. Individuals in this state are sapped of their strength, and will, many times, lose the will to continue pushing forward, seeing the world through a lens of darkness that lacks emotion. They will see no reason behind whatever they do, and go through life mechanically.

This feeling can later translate to either suicidal thoughts or the very act of suicide, and so it is necessary to face this problem now, before it becomes full-blown in society and the whole world is overwhelmed by another crisis—this time, an existential one.

Chapter Three

FAMILY UNDER LOCKDOWN

Other things may change us, but we start and end with the family. —**Anthony Brandt**

Typical pre-pandemic family ecosystems were powered by strict routines that ran like clockwork. Two-parent households saw each parent performing certain roles that ranged from domestic, financial, emotional, and even spiritual pursuits. Children also had their own duties to perform as a way of contributing to the home, including staying on top of their schoolwork.

Single-parent households had pretty much the same mode of operation, with parents and children knowing what things were expected of them and doing their best to meet up to these expectations.

Then, without warning, the pandemic struck, sweeping up everything in its path with the same mercilessness as a hurricane. Many things were affected; and among these things was regular family dynamics. There is no disputing that the moment the stay-at-home order was issued by the government, all families struggled to adjust.

The usual school runs were no longer required, as students had to attend their classes from home. Daycare centers were shut down, so the parents with toddlers had to figure out a way to fit caring for their child into their busy schedules. Apart from parents who were essential workers, those who still had jobs after the lockdown had to find office space within the home. And, all these dilemmas would have to be resolved while still catering to the household and its requirements.

Confusion was the automatic reaction. Like dice being thrown, family routines were shaken up and fingers were crossed for the best outcomes. Parents had to go back to the drawing board to come up with novel parenting techniques to maintain sanity in their households, and normal day-to-day activities were thrown out the window to make room for new ones.

All families were not affected the same way, though. Some had it easier than most. Or harder. In the rare case where a family had home-schooled kids and parents that worked from or at home, the stay-at-home order was not a dreadful thing, even though it was due to a deadly virus.

For parents that did not already work from home, trying to wrap their heads around not being able to go into the office was tricky and frustrating—but not more frustrating than those who had no job at all.

Being forced to spend days on end with family turned out to be a blessing for some and a bane for others. A number of families began to realize that there is only a thin line between quality time and too much time. COVID-19, the new sheriff in town, put families on their toes. There was no option for them than to get on with their programs. Everything they were used to would no longer suffice, if they wanted their family to survive these times. Different aspects of family life needed to be addressed and tweaked, where necessary; like responsibilities, communication, mental health, income, education, and more.

Nonetheless, the lockdown order yielded both positive and negative outcomes in families; and we will delve into these two categories.

NEGATIVE EFFECTS OF THE PANDEMIC ON FAMILIES

- **Loss of Income/Low Income**

One of the main aspects of family life affected during the COVID-19 pandemic was income streams. Families have a specific income that they run on, and this was challenged by the pandemic and the loss of jobs. When the pandemic struck, many companies had to shut down indefinitely or permanently, sending these income earners away with nothing to fall back on. There were very few opportunities for those who had no educational qualifications and depended on daily wages, and some parents had no choice but to take salary cuts, as their companies were struggling to stay afloat.

Low-income families bore the brunt of this unfortunate situation. Children and parents from low-income families were already lacking in social opportunities. Those families who were already on a strict budget to keep food on the table and a roof over their heads could no longer afford to do so.

Family dynamics were also affected as a result of the pressure of quickly-depleting resources. Stress, frustration, and anxiety levels were at an all-time high. Many parents struggled to keep it together to avoid letting their children sense the tension brimming beneath the surface while children, not knowing any better, continued to badger their parents for their needs.

Childrens' developments were affected by this loss of income. Parent-child interactions were reduced to a minimum, and soon, relationships between family members and even partners (parents) became strained.

Job opportunities have begun to increase, post-lockdown, and a few of these families have started to find their footing again. Being able to go out has given these families the hope of a better tomorrow and a less intense atmosphere in which to repair their frail relationships.

- **Poor Mental Health**

This is one of the biggest battles the world has had to fight, especially as mental health struggles in young adults and children have been on the rise in recent times. Young people were especially at risk of deteriorating mental states, as they could not fully understand the pandemic.

Many young people already found coping mechanisms within their day-to-day activities, and the loss of their routines impacted their mental health negatively. What started as confusion soon evolved into aggressive behaviour by these children, as a response to feeling overwhelmed and boxed in.

With the number of infected and dead on the rise, children were also anxious about contracting the disease or passing it on to their family members. Forced solitude was scary for the families of those with severe mental health issues because they lived in constant fear that these youngsters might opt for harmful solutions to ease the pain.

In low-income families, children could not help but sense their parents' difficulty and feel guilty, as a result. Parents themselves were not exempt from mental health struggles as many of them teetered back and forth on the brink of depression and had to try extra hard to keep it together for their children.

These families had never been happier than after the lockdown was eased. Parents are now able to get much-needed professional help for themselves and their children and, slowly but steadily, life is going back to normal.

- **Too Much Family Time**

Even close-knit families found the lockdown to be a true test of their bonds. In families whose relationships were already hanging by a thread, being forced to spend hours on end with each other was the straw that broke the camel's back.

The lockdown was a time when negative feelings were common. Because not everyone is able to control their feelings, some families had to deal with these emotions spilling out from different family members, creating a toxic home environment.

The friction was palpable. Parents couldn't control their outbursts because they, too, were frustrated by the situation, especially in low-income homes. Children, also, were forced to respond with the same level of frustration, as they were dealing with their own issues.

Relationships have not been spared during the lockdown. Couples that had been considering breaking up finally grabbed the bull by the horns. In July 2020, LegalTemplates, a leading contract-creation site, posted, "…we've seen a 34% increase in sales of our divorce agreement, compared to the same period in 2019."

Despite the challenges, not all relationships and families fell apart. Some chose to hang on to see if anything would change post-lockdown; and now they are currently working on repairing those frail bonds between them.

- **Domestic Violence**

The lockdown was a horrendous time for victims of domestic and gender-based violence. Before COVID-19, it was estimated that one in three women will experience violence during their lifetimes. Less than 40% of women who are domestic violence (DV) victims reached out for help. But, there was a surge in the reports of domestic violence cases reaching healthcare and justice service providers.

It is speculated that the anger and frustration caused by financial troubles have exacerbated the anger and stress levels of these aggressors. And there was nowhere for their victims to flee to. In countries like Colombia, DV reports spiked a whopping 225% in the first week of the pandemic. In India, the National Commission for Women (NCW) registered 587 DV complaints between March 23rd and April 16th. During the first two weeks of lockdown in Nigeria, violence among partners increased from 364 in March to 794 in April.

Women are not the only victims of DV. Children and men experience it, too. Mothers and fathers also let their frustrations lead them to hit their children; and in rare cases, men were abused by their partners.

While there is no excuse for hostile and violent behaviour, there is also no disputing that the lockdown contributed greatly to this increased aggression.

The numbers of DV reports have begun to lower once more, and there is now hope that, with growing awareness and support for domestic violence victims, abusive responses will become a thing of the past.

- **Remote Working/Schooling**

In low-income families and countries, working and schooling remotely was a most inconvenient thing. Not many families are able to afford gadgets for every member of the household, and not all homes are able to pay for high-speed internet, due to limited financial resources. These two problems had to be solved, somehow.

Some families had one or two computers. Every weekday during the lockdown, it was the job of the parents to choose whether their children would log in to attend classes that day, or if they would log in for work, instead. The outcome of this crucial decision would be detrimental, either way, because it meant that somebody had to miss out.

As a result, children were behind their peers, and some had to opt out of remote schooling entirely because they did not have the means to participate. It was the same thing for parents: some had to resign or were let go from their jobs because they could not meet the new demands. Even those who lost their jobs could not get new ones, because they could not fulfill the requirements of having a readily available computer and high-speed internet to work seamlessly from home.

This situation made parents feel inadequate and caused children to blame their parents for their dropping grades. For these families, it was a great relief when the lockdown was eased and children were allowed to go back to school.

- **Increased Screen Time**

There used to be a battle between screen time and the outside world, but the pandemic came around and declared a winner. There was no other way to interact with people except with the use of the internet. Remote learning and working were the first reasons for increased screen time for children and parents, respectively—but this wasn't so bad because it was necessary screen time, right?

After a long day of working or schooling, there was nothing left to do. Families tried to create activities around the home that would keep them off their screens, but people still needed to interact with the outside world, using apps like Zoom for work calls and Facetime for calls with friends.

Experts have said that there isn't really any cause to worry. It was to be expected, since there was no option to just go outside. But, as it turns out, with or without a pandemic, when your child spends too much time gaming or scrolling mindlessly through social media to the point where it affects their daily functioning, it can be a sign of depression. And this number spiked during the pandemic.

The challenges parents had to face was creating a healthy balance and figuring out the reason for spending too much time staring at computer screens. After all, parents, too, spent hours on streaming platforms like Netflix, Hulu, and Youtube, to pass the time.

It is the job of the parent to make sure their children finish their schoolwork and chores before getting engrossed with these devices, and to create restrictions on the things they watch and the time they spend on their devices.

- **Loss of loved ones**

The pandemic also took many lives due to Covid, natural causes, or even suicide. Covid guidelines prohibited many from being with their sick family members in the last moments of their lives, and this was a hard pill to swallow.

The social distancing protocols also meant that they had to find ways to grieve without going through the normal process of gaining closure. Funerals were not allowed, and the dead had to be cremated or kept in the morgues to curb the spread of the virus. A large number of families lost their elderly members, as they were most vulnerable due to their weakened immune systems. Some people had to deal both with losing their parents and explaining to their kids that Covid was the reason their grandparent was no more.

The recent availability of vaccines was like re-opening new wounds. Many families grieved anew, wishing the vaccines had been released earlier so that their loved ones could be alive today.

- **Bad Habits/Addiction**

There's something about bad habits that make them too easy to form, and the lockdown did not help, in this department. Since the routines people were so used to had fallen apart, they had to find a way to fill those extra hours with activities; and, for many, what started as one day of being carefree would turn into months of addiction.

All habits have lingering effects. The difference between bad and good habits is that the effects of the bad ones are usually detrimental, even though they might not seem like it at the time.

When the lockdown started, families did not know what to do. So, they winged it. They had no plans, no schedules, and nothing to keep them accountable to themselves. Days passed without accomplishing anything. This was the easiest bad habit to form, because it did not appear to be a bad habit at all.

The stress, depression, and anxiety caused by the lockdown led both parents and their children to bad coping methods like binge eating unhealthy comfort foods, daily drinking (even in the daytime), smoking and vaping, and the use of hard drugs. Some of the more mindless habits are a sedentary lifestyle (too much use of social media, gaming, online gambling, watching TV all day long, online shopping, and excessive pornography and masturbation).

Post-lockdown families now have to work towards quitting these addictions, even though going back outside has given them little time to indulge. Family members must help each other let go of these harmful acts and be accountable to one another, on this journey.

POSITIVE EFFECTS OF THE PANDEMIC ON FAMILIES

- **Improved Communication**

The first hurdle parents experienced was explaining the pandemic to children—a situation they were still grappling to understand themselves. Younger children had more questions, and the younger the child, the more painstaking the explanation as to how a virus could spread so fast that staying indoors was the only way to minimize its spread. Children also had to be educated on the need for face masks and social distancing, and all these lessons had to be imparted while assuaging their fears and helping them adjust.

As a result, many families had to devise new and more efficient communication strategies to help their children (and themselves) understand the situation and cope with it.

Typically, in most families, parents and their children communicated very little due to the age/generation gap, and the fast-paced nature of their lives made this type of communication even easier to avoid. But the pandemic slowed down time and created more avenues for actual interactions between family members.

Some families saw this as an opportunity to learn better ways to express frustration. Instead of frequent outbursts of anger, parents and children learned to speak to one another with civility and respect. Conflict resolution skills in families have also improved since the pandemic hit. But, to make this happen, parents had to prove that it was safe for their children to come to them with things that weighed heavily on their minds, and children also had to learn to be forthcoming with their worries.

In those families who have taken the time to bridge the communication gap, life after quarantine has improved by a mile. Angry outbursts are fewer, and family members, especially children, can now speak freely and without fear of chastisement.

This was easy to accomplish once they realized it just required listening and speaking kindly, honestly, reassuringly, and with empathy (including physical touch, when necessary).

- **Remote Working/Schooling**

Families with the resources (stable internet, electricity, and gadgets) to carry out remote activities seamlessly had no qualms in adopting to this new style of living. Parents in these homes believed that this new home schooling method worked better for them and their children, as the one-on-one, hands-on approach led to the faster development of language skills—including reading and writing. Parents were able to keep an eye on their children to spot their strengths and weaknesses, and intervened when they seemed to be overwhelmed.

These parents also found it more convenient to work from home, as not having to dress up and spend hours in traffic, after getting their children ready for school, proved to be better for productivity.

New jobs have been created as a result of the need for working from home. For some parents, things are looking up, as they have been able to land jobs from any part of the world without having to worry about commuting (or, worse, relocating).

- **Quality Family Time**

Before the lockdown, family members barely had any spare time to spend together, so many families seized the quarantine period to enjoy and make the best of their time together, engaging in activities that strengthened their familial bonds.

Working from home gave parents who had not been able to spend quality time with their newborns and young children time to participate in their upbringing; especially in the years where they are most impressionable.

For mothers of newborns, it also helped that their husbands were available to care for the children, since fathers are usually given only two weeks of paternity leave. The equal parenting opportunity created by the lockdown helped to boost the confidence of these fathers, allowing them to participate in their child's day-to-day milestones while their children could still recognize and bond with them.

The lockdown provided ample time for activities that seemed a luxury before the pandemic, like having meals together or sharing experiences in the evening, after a long day. Families also experimented with different activities like watching TV shows together, cooking, doing chores together, playing games, and even learning new a skill.

The lockdown was also a good time to rekindle relationships with extended family members, both virtually and in real life. Family members who had not been able to keep up with one another due to distance and the stress of day-to-day living now had the opportunity to catch up.

Ironically, mandatory isolation brought family members, far and near, closer together. To this day, some families still look back at the lockdown fondly, because going back outside meant that things would go back to the way they were before COVID-19. Still, these newly-revived relationships have outlasted the lockdown, and those who took advantage of the pandemic in this way are endlessly grateful that they did.

- **More Rest Time**

The realization that life before the pandemic was almost too hectic dawned on many when the lockdown finally began. Many of us had never believed in enjoying the little things that life had in store for us until the pandemic came around and forced us to pay attention to ourselves and the needs of others.

The pandemic freed up schedules and gave people much extra time—more than they knew what to do with. This meant that all the hours not usually accounted for, like time spent in transit or traffic, pretty much became 'resting time'.

Parents and their children could take longer hours to rest privately, after spending time together. Those who barely got 8 hours of sleep every day (which is important to the long-term wellbeing of the human body) were grateful for the extra hours of sleep.

Family members picked up healthy relaxation practices like meditation and cleaning and decluttering personal spaces, which is therapeutic. This also included other activities such as yoga, workouts, journaling, and taking long, soothing baths to relax the mind and body—activities which they could either do together, or separately.

- **Good Habits**

Before the lockdown, the hustle and bustle in our daily lives was a common excuse for procrastination. This changed after the pandemic began. It was as though the 'perfect time' everyone had been waiting for had finally arrived, in all its glory.

Research has shown that it takes 18 to 254 days to form habits. This means that, for those who had truly wished they had more time, there was no hesitation in finally kicking bad habits to the curb, or starting and maintaining those life-changing good habits.

One such habit is exercise and fitness. Especially for parents, embarking on a fitness journey required time that they could not afford to spare. The lockdown handed them a good opportunity to start working out until it became second nature to them. Other habits that were formed included healthy living practices like yoga, meditation, and cleaning.

Another habit that many cultivated as a result of the pandemic was washing hands and a better attention to overall hygiene in the home.

Children and parents could also devote time to the hobbies they had shoved aside before, either as a group or individually. Many families and family members also intensified their spiritual pursuits. Mentally stimulating habits like reading and journaling were cultivated in others.

- **Responsibilities**

The responsibility of caring for the home shifted. Many family members had to re-evaluate their contribution to the family and homes. Old roles had to be discarded and replaced by new ones. For instance, most families that had one person filling the role of homemaker now had all hands on deck. Parents assumed part of the responsibility of teaching to ensure that their children did their schoolwork, as that remained the most important thing.

The task fell on parents to teach their children life skills, and they accomplished this by assigning them responsibilities around the home. Parents who did not give their children tasks to perform around the house now saw the importance of doing so, regardless of a child's age. Chores can differ with age, from personal responsibilities like cleaning rooms and making the beds to, as they get older, bigger tasks like sweeping, doing the dishes, and taking the trash out.

This new way of splitting responsibilities helps equip children with the skills they need to live independently in the future. Sharing responsibilities has even helped parents stay more accountable to each other.

- **Improved Emotional Intelligence/Empathy**

Michael J. Fox said, "Family is not an important thing. It's everything," and the lockdown was instrumental in helping family members understand this. In many families, there has been a positive shift in family dynamics since then, after the lockdown allowed for a recollection and renewal of the bonds they share.

Family members having to interact more intimately and frequently with one another bolstered the emotional keenness in these individuals. With better communication, many have learned to appreciate the quirks and differences in others that make them who they are. Parents reduced the amount of pressure on kids, and children, in turn, put a leash on the rebels within them.

The real eye-opener was the personal struggles that many people had to deal with during the pandemic. The vulnerability added an extra layer of humanness to us, and we were able to see others through a different lens. Since people wanted to be treated with kindness, they saw that they had to reciprocate the empathy that they sought.

This emotional intelligence has extended past the borders of family, as we see in our society today. People have become kinder and more outspoken towards injustices perpetrated against other people from different backgrounds. And, hopefully, this new way will persist long after the pandemic becomes history.

TIPS TO FOSTER FAMILIAL BONDS

Hopefully, the lockdown is long behind us, but we can't deny that its aftershock still reverberates in the present. Reintegrating into society takes its own toll, and it might be easy to get carried away by the new changes and neglect the family. So, listed below are a few tips that can help bolster familial relationships.

- Continue to communicate. Whether or not family members still work/school from home, talk about your day with the members of your family, and listen to their stories.

- Create family time, no matter how tight schedules are. Eat meals as a family, play games, pray, and watch shows together.

- Speak with kindness and practice empathy.
- Make time for self-care.
- Keep up the good habits. Eat healthy, and exercise.
- Seek professional help for yourself or family members who need it.
- Look for reasons to be grateful together and for each other.
- Offer support to one another as you navigate new phases in your lives.

Chapter Four

LOVE UNDER LOCKDOWN

There is never a time or place for true love. It happens accidentally, in a heartbeat, in a single flashing, throbbing moment. **—Sarah Dessen**

No matter how small or big an object is, when you view it with a magnifying glass, you will discover new or hidden features that you never knew were there. For romantic relationships in 2020, the lockdown was the magnifying glass through which people experienced their relationships anew.

For starters, single people in search of partners surrendered to the idea that dating had to be halted for a while, and proceeded to wait until the pandemic ended to continue their search.

For people with partners, sustaining romantic relationships before the pandemic was already no walk in the park. But COVID-19 still showed up and forced us indoors, where we had all the time in the world to cross-examine everything we thought we knew about ourselves, love, and relationships.

2020 will always be a memorable one, because it was the year human relationships of all kinds took a hit, and romantic relationships were not left out. For some, the new perspective was that thing they never knew they'd needed, and it gave their relationship a firmer structure. But, people experienced the pandemic in different ways, and for many, this new perspective turned out to be quite disruptive to their relationship dynamics.

The same pandemic that forced families to live closer together under the same roof split some families, cities, states, and even countries apart. The rapid lifestyle switch caused by the lockdown sent stress levels through the roof. The expected fear and panic visited everyone and made too many individuals feel vulnerable, and at their rawest. And since too much of anything always turns out to be bad (whether this 'anything' is purportedly positive or negative), things were mostly not good in the world of romantic relationships.

The turn of events left the whole world with limited options. It had suddenly become survival mode. Couples forced to spend the quarantine either together or separately had different sets of problems to deal with.

THE NEGATIVE EFFECTS OF LOCKDOWN ON ROMANTIC RELATIONSHIPS

Regardless of how healthy the relationship is, all the numerous possible relationship dynamics—whether in long distance, married, unmarried, cohabiting, or brand-new relationships—were strained due to the pandemic. There were some unsavoury outcomes, and a few of them are explained below.

- **Domestic Violence**

DV is one of the biggest human rights violations. The European Institute for Gender Equality says, "Both women and men experience gender-based violence, but the majority of victims are women and girls."

Forced confinement gave room for animosity to brew and this, in turn, caused the rate of gender-based violence, especially against women, to increase.

According to an analysis by the National Commission on COVID-19 and Criminal Justice (NCCCJ), the number of domestic violence incidents in the US increased by 8.1% after lockdown orders. Calls to domestic violence hotlines also increased. This meant that, for these victims of domestic abuse, the home became their prison. It was akin to putting predator and prey in the same cage, with no means of escape.

The reasons for this spike are numerous, with the likeliest overarching factor being frustration; whether from loss of jobs or income or the abrupt lifestyle change caused by the compulsory quarantine.

Another likely reason for this spike in the number of domestic violence cases around the world is the increase in the use of alcohol or drugs as a coping mechanism.

The vulnerable women and men who had been badly hurt found it difficult to get help during the lockdown because not only were they stuck, but hospitals were also a huge risk, as they were serving as the battlefront for the war against COVID, and emergency call centers had a lot on their plates with the deluge of calls being received. So, as a result, many countries set up more hotlines so victims could call in and get the help they needed.

- **Depreciating Mental Health**

Everybody has a responsibility to look out for their own mental health. But, in the year of the lockdown, it became so much more difficult to stay sane.

Couples who did not live together would no longer be able to meet each other for a while. For all couples, especially married or cohabiting, a poor state of mind for one person invariably meant some sort of disruption to the partner's mental or emotional state. Anxiety and shock from being confined indoors with the same person for months on end, or not being able to spend any time with their significant other, put many couples in a tough spot, made harder in homes where there were children to care for.

While it is good to offer support to those struggling with mental health, it becomes increasingly hectic for the person solely pulling the emotional weight of the relationship.

The symptoms of depression and anxiety (loss of interest in daily activities, apathy, low energy levels, and mood swings—a nightmare for both parties) are not easy to navigate, and it is even harder for those who have never experienced it, or have their own mental health issues to take care of.

In lockdown relationships, cohabiting or otherwise, partners had to learn to cope or, in worst case scenarios, had no other choice but to walk away from the relationship.

- **Fear and Panic**

There is no denying that the abrupt switch from hustle and bustle to mandatory quarantine was not only shocking, but also scary. The videos circulating the internet and news of people in critical conditions fighting for their lives did nothing to help assuage these fears.

Then the daily updates on the number of positive cases and deaths became the icing on the cake. For those who struggled with health anxiety, the hypochondriac in them kicked into overdrive with every update.

The partners of these people had to deal with either of these factors: their significant other's fear of getting the virus, or the panic that they had finally contracted the virus, every time they felt something off. Some people even went so far as to isolate themselves from their partner in the same home, as an extra precaution. And this usually included an unwillingness to be intimate.

This reaction, of course, would put a dent in any relationship, as constant intimacy in any form is important to its sustenance. This withdrawal will lead to the other partner feeling rejected and unloved, and will take the relationship down the path of destruction.

- **Poor Finances**

Unfortunately, many homes experienced a loss of income because of the lockdown. Even with the palliative provisions by governments, these homes were barely sustaining.

The shortage of money brought on by the loss of jobs or income sources made individuals feel inadequate and angry. Those feelings were reflected in the interactions of couples dealing with financial problems, and these abrasive interactions in turn impacted mental health, self-esteem, and the relationship, overall.

- **Poor Communication**

One would expect that the lockdown would allow for easier and more frequent communication between couples, especially those living together. But, this was not always the case.

The lockdown brought with it many shifts to the communication dynamics of pre-existing relationships and exacerbated individual stress levels. Being apart or around each other too much made it extremely hard to get a handle on communication patterns. So, couples had to strike a balance between over-communicating or under-communicating.

Humans are social beings, so the heightened feelings of being confined and restricted from outside communication led to miscommunication. Individuals either tended to hold back their feelings too much until they finally broke and let out violent outbursts, or were too outspoken about their feelings, and the words they spoke were hurtful or vile.

- **Sex life**

A study on the changes in sexuality and the quality of couple relationships during the lockdown in Italy stated, "Despite the pandemic's psychological consequences, when asked directly, most couples responded that they did not perceive any differences in their sexuality. However, some female participants did report a decrease in pleasure, satisfaction, desire, and arousal. The main reasons behind the changes in sexuality in women, therefore, appear to be worry, lack of privacy, and stress."

Those whose sex lives were impacted during the pandemic found it was due to several reasons, including exhaustion from the new lifestyle, depression or mental stress, low self-esteem brought on by post-lockdown weight gain, the plethora of feelings brought on by the lockdown, or the lack of time or space to carry out these intimate acts, among other things.

***

But the pandemic also brought with it an opportunity: the chance to resolve and reconcile. There was ample time for those who were always on the move to sit down and gradually seek closure. So, while it seemed like there was mostly trouble in paradise, it was *really* a period for couples to finally address all the elephants in their rooms and decide the best steps to take for all involved.

However, even as the restrictions are being lifted, it is still a bit awkward to re-transition to life before the pandemic, and couples will need each other as they realize that life after the pandemic is similar, but not the same as the experiences we are accustomed to and expect.

HOW TO NAVIGATE LOVE UNDER LOCKDOWN

A healthy relationship is not one that is devoid of the occasional argument or highs and lows. It is one where the good days outweigh the bad, without any form of abuse, and partners are intentional about each other and themselves.

The healthiest relationships have their off days, too. Here are tips to help you manage your relationship through the strain of the lockdown.

- **Accept and Adapt**

Coming to terms with the new reality is important, if partners are going to be able to stay sane through these times. Couples must accept that things will no longer be the same as they used to be, and will have to find new methods to keep their ships sailing.

Having to live differently than you are used to can expose the vulnerabilities you have worked hard to conceal. The new way of life sheds a new light on personalities as people begin to spend more time with themselves and learn things they did not know about themselves. Acceptance here means acceptance of yourself as an individual, of each other, the relationship, and your new reality; while adapting means making tasty lemonade even though the lemons handed to you are terribly sour.

Accepting and adapting does not mean that you will not experience stress and challenges along the way. It just means that you are ready to face them head-on. Anxiety-filled days will still come your way and some days your partner will not be the easiest to deal with; but accepting your situation with all the fear and uncertainty it presents will give you a bit of an upper hand.

- **Make plans**

Before the pandemic, people had planned out their days, weeks, and even years. Most people live by routines, and this became obvious when our routines were disrupted by the stay-at-home order. This also meant that the one thing most people had in common during the lockdown was figuring out what to do with all the spare time that was handed to them by the pandemic.

Making plans is a good way to take care of yourself and declutter your mind. Of course, plans do not have to be elaborate or include going outside, but they can be as simple as having a set time to wake up, workout, eat breakfast, take a shower, wear clean clothes, and go about your work for the day. Doing routines just like you used to every day before the pandemic makes a world of difference.

Couples should plan their day individually, but also so that they have activities that intersect. For those in long-distance relationships, making plans also includes making time in the day to communicate through regular updates to your partner.

Planning your day also eases the burden of depending on a partner too much, or requiring them to spend all their time with you. You can be productive, set small personal goals, and crush them even in the face of the pandemic.

- **Pay Attention to Mental Health**

The Kaiser Family Foundation analyzed a report from the US Census Bureau and reported that, "During the COVID-19 pandemic, concerns about mental health and substance use have grown, including concerns about suicidal ideation. In January 2021, 41% of adults reported symptoms of anxiety and/or depressive disorder, a share that has been largely stable since spring 2020. In a survey from June 2020, 13% of adults reported new or increased substance use due to coronavirus-related stress, and 11% of adults reported thoughts of suicide in the past 30 days. Suicide rates have long been on the rise and may worsen due to the pandemic."

This report shows that more people than you know are struggling with mental health issues—and your partner could be one of them. The lockdown made many people start to feel self-conscious, unhappy, anxious, or depressed; especially those who had lost jobs or income sources.

When you have a partner whose mental state is taking a turn for the worse, understand that taking care of your partner's mental health is very important to having a healthy relationship, so do not undermine or invalidate their worries. Be empathetic, encourage them to let you in, help them find healthy coping mechanisms, and seek professional help if it seems like there is cause for alarm.

- **Meditate**

The fear of the coronavirus can be so grave that it begins to affect your functioning and also your relationships. One way to ease these fears is by picking up the habit of meditation.

The art of meditation involves learning how to train your mind to focus and channel your thoughts in a specific direction. Meditation is a good therapy to alleviate stress. It also helps you become more aware of yourself and surroundings.

Meditation is done by sitting still for at least 15 minutes and controlling your breathing. There are a million and one in-depth resources on the internet that you can use as you embark on your meditation journey. They will guide you as you work to make your relationship better.

- **Interact with Civility**

It is easy for you to get carried away by the barrage of emotions that come with adjusting to a new life, then be tempted to take it out on your partner.

The ability to stay cool under pressure is one you must hone and nurture in order to be able to keep an amicable relationship with your partner, and this applies across all categories of romantic relationships. Whether further apart or closer together, couples should practice respectful interactions. Be civil and careful about the words being hurled at one other, especially when tempers flare.

A genial atmosphere will give room for both parties to be themselves, promoting interactions and conflicts that are healthy and which will not end in hurtful words being exchanged, or abuse taking place.

Your partner is not responsible for the current situation of things, so do not take it out on them. Everyone deserves a partner who treats them with utmost respect and civility.

- **Respect Boundaries**

The concept of personal space became even clearer after the lockdown began. The pandemic was automatically a stressful situation, and it caused many people, even those who preferred living together with their significant others, to have second thoughts about cohabiting.

Not many people have mansions to retreat into to enjoy unlimited space, and so had to resign themselves to the fate they had been presented with. Cohabiting couples with kids in the picture had even less personal space than they did before, since there was no way they could avoid bumping into one another.

Boundary issues have become more rampant since the lockdown. A good trick to curb issues like these is to know your boundaries and set them, as well.

There needs to be mutual understanding between you and your partner on the need for 'me time'. Spending a little time apart, even when in the same house or outside of it, gives you more excitement when you see each other again, and plenty to discuss. Do not nag or complain about little things all the time.

Also, not all the boundaries that need to be drawn are physical boundaries. Some of them are mental. Mental boundaries also mean taking time for personal development and doing things like meditating, reading, watching movies, or yoga—activities that calm the mind.

- **Practice Gratitude**

The act of gratitude makes everything more bearable. Gratitude means finding goodness in the people and things around you. It is a powerful weapon that, when wielded, changes your perspective and makes you remain positive no matter the situation. There is also an attractive force around gratitude: the more grateful you are, the more the universe keeps giving you things to be grateful for.

Starting a gratitude lifestyle is easy. Simply speak or write about the things you are grateful for at every chance you get. You can start a gratitude journal, where you write about the people and things you are grateful for (especially your partner and relationship, in this peculiar case).

- **Staying positive**

The plethora of negative emotions will keep coming, but it is your job to keep them at bay. One trick to staying positive is being careful with the information you consume from the internet, as there is an abundance of frightening and false information there.

Also, develop a routine that keeps you grounded. Do not sweep your feelings under the rug—allow yourself to feel them. Learn new skills or hobbies to keep your mind preoccupied, and make time every day to talk to the ones you love; especially your partner.

- **Spice Up Your Sex Life**

The anxiety and depression that characterized the lockdown period made it hard on a couples' intimacy. At first, it seemed like this would be smooth sailing (spending all that time with your significant other). But, after going through many emotional rough patches and handling domestic responsibilities all day long, the last thing on you or your partner's mind might be lovemaking.

Some partners were able to keep being intimate through it all, but others were not so fortunate, whether due to distance or because they no longer felt desire for sexual relations, like they used to. If you belong in the latter category, you must understand that this lack of desire does not mean that there is anything wrong with you or your partner, and thus sex will not be the same as before.

The perks of having sex are numerous, but two key positives are that it is good for cardiovascular health, and it also facilitates the release of endorphins which help lower the levels of anxiety or depression.

For these reasons, you should try to sustain a sex life between you and your partner. There are many things you can do to reawaken your sex life.

First, remain flirty. Act like lovestruck teenagers every chance you get. Dress up attractively and use perfume, because many scents stimulate libido. Touch and kiss each other randomly. Before lovemaking, spend time on foreplay, as this improves the quality of sex.

Set up romantic activities that you can do indoors, like food or movie dates. Light candles to set the mood (some scented candles have aphrodisiac effects). But also, most importantly, practice self-care; because the only way you can give or receive pleasure from your partner is if you already feel pleased with yourself.

- **Be Empathetic and Thoughtful**

The disruptions that came with the pandemic were overwhelming and rattled even the most emotionally grounded. Almost everyone experienced some level of difficulty dealing with anxiety in one way or another.

There has been no better time to show empathy. Interestingly, showing empathy to others helps you have a better handle on your feelings and on the reality of the world. Not only does empathizing with others show them that they are not alone, but it helps you feel the same way, too.

Some ways to show empathy to your partner is by listening to them; especially when they have a lot of worries on their mind, and demonstrating thoughtfulness by performing random acts of service. If empathy does not come easily to you, you can be intentional about getting better by studying how others display empathy and putting yourself in others' shoes.

Other thoughtful acts are giving homemade gifts, or buying things online that they want. Random love massages after a long day can go a long way towards giving your partner relief. You can also help them with chores, or make them meals if they have a penchant for food.

All these acts might seem small, but they can make all the difference.

- **Do Fun Activities Together**

Giving each other personal space is great, because everyone needs time to recharge, but a great relationship is one where both parties have mastered the art of friendship.

Spontaneity is one way to have fun. Sometimes, just ignore the routine and wing it, for that day. Discard any daily activities that you can do without, and allow yourselves a day off. You can also plan activities that you would not normally do, like hiking, indoor picnics, or even outdoor picnics (while obeying social distancing rules).

You can also play games together—board games, video games, or crossword puzzles. Cook together, share memes with each other, or hop on social media challenges for couples to pass the time and have a little fun. Attend virtual birthdays, weddings, or baby shower parties together. For those separated by distance, arrange virtual dates where you both dress and eat meals or watch movies together.

You can also have shared routines—activities you have agreed to only do together. For instance, you can find a movie series on Hulu or Netflix that matches both your preferences, or start a couple's workout.

To bond as a couple, partners must have activities that they partake in together. These activities will help both of you to take the edge off, get in a few laughs, and distract you from the worries on your minds.

- **Communicate Efficiently**

There was so much widespread internal turmoil to deal with during the lockdown that many people found it easier to keep their worries to themselves instead of burdening others with them. But, relationships can only survive when the parties involved communicate often and efficiently.

If there is distance between the both of you, do not allow that to hinder your communication. Communicating does not have to be face-to-face to hold water.

Telling your partner how you are feeling is relevant at all times, even with more unsavoury emotions like anger or sadness (though they are more difficult to express). When there is a conversation that needs to be had, one must first process all the things that are being felt, to ensure clarity of thought before going ahead with the conversation.

When talking, avoid mincing words or making generic statements. Use your words, but remember to speak calmly. Address only the matter in question, and do not be in a hurry to insinuate about or invalidate what you think your partner is feeling. Also, don't jump to defend yourself when they are pointing out a wrong that you may have done to them. Learn the art of listening, and only speak when you must.

Avoid passive-aggressive behaviour. Pick a time where there is no rage, and make sure that the end goal of every conversation is to resolve the problem. Finally, communication is mostly verbal, but talking is not the only way to communicate. You can write notes or send texts if you feel like the time is not right for face-to-face talks. Or, give your partner something they love in the form of a peace offering to help calm them down enough to have a conversation.

***

Coronavirus and the lockdown changed many lives; some for better and others for worse. The storm has passed, and love under lockdown seems to be a thing of the past, but many of these practices that began during the quarantine should not be hastily discarded because, lockdown or not, being in a relationship takes work and intentionality.

Chapter Five

THE PANDEMIC AND THE ECONOMY

Only a strong economy can create higher asset values and sustainability good returns for savers"
—Ben Bernanke.

The pandemic affected all facets of our lives, and the economy wasn't excluded. The virus spread with alarming speed like a wildfire, infecting a lot of people and bringing the economy to an involuntary standstill. National economies took a hit, businesses closed down, and people were forced out of their jobs. What made the negative impact of the pandemic worse is that no one saw it coming. No one prepared for it, and so many businesses, especially small-scale operations, did not have a crisis management plan.

The strain on the economy forced the government to begin to devise measures to revive the failing economy, as well as find means to curb the spread of the virus. However, despite the efforts of the government in this area, another variant of the virus is already spreading as I write. It is as if the virus is intent on waging a war against humanity.

***

It all began with supply shortages, which affected a couple of sectors due to impulse and panic buying and the heightened usage of some goods to fight the pandemic. There were also instances of price extortion. On the 24th of February, 2020, the global stock markets fell due to a significant rise in the number of COVID-19 cases. By February, the global stock market would be hit by the largest single-week declines since the 2008 financial crisis. It eventually crashed in March 2020.

The global tourism and aviation industry suffered a large share of the hit, too. This is because one major way to curb the spread of the virus is to stop global movement. This led to a halt in their activities.

The hospitality sector, as well, was hit hard, with millions of jobs lost and many companies going bankrupt. As there was a shutdown in the aviation sector, there was also a massive shutdown in hotels and rental buildings all over the world, with reservations falling abruptly.

However, despite the havoc that the pandemic wrecked on businesses and industries globally, it was not just a tale of gloom through and through.

Take the music industry, for example. While shows and concerts were cancelled, the ingenuity of humans to create new possibilities emerged. Some musicians were able to make music videos in their homes. One example is the music video 'Stuck With You' by Justin Bieber and Arianne Grande, even though it was not as perfect as a physical event with interpersonal interactions.

This was the same in the film industry, as most actors made personal short videos (with their families) and uploaded them on several internet sites such as YouTube, Instagram, Facebook, and the like. This made it obvious that the reason why these industries gained stability (at least, to some extent) is because of the 'Power of Technology'. All of these reasons have an impact on the content itself.

Research has shown that songs are getting shorter and snappier, mainly in response to the need to boost the number of individual plays. Other players are adapting much as Tsai Chun Pan describes: "The short video is a new entertainment model. This model has a huge demand for music content, which has not only brought us many new opportunities but also provided us with a new content promotion and distribution channel." TikTok, already changing how consumers discover music, is developing its own streaming service that is expected to contribute to these evolving dynamics.

Checking into the 'business of music', it becomes clear that "the pandemic is truly a leveler, leaving no stone or sector unaffected," as I said earlier.

Unemployment As Well As Massive Layoffs: Yet Another Difficult Year for Job Seekers

Of all aspects of social misery, nothing is as heartbreaking as unemployment. —Jane Addams

Many people have lost their jobs or seen their incomes cut. Unemployment rates have increased in all major countries. As a result, the world economy struggles with rising unemployment. In the United States, the proportion of people out of work hit a yearly total of 8.9%, according to the International Monetary Fund (IMF), signaling an end to a decade of job expansion.

Job vacancies in Australia have returned to the same level as of 2019, but they are lagging in France, Spain, the UK, and several other countries. Job vacancies or opportunities are still very low in many countries.

Eleanor Roosevelt once said: "Everyone has the right to work; to free choice of employment; to just and favourable conditions of work; and to protect against unemployment."

It is not news that there are many unemployed people around the world, especially in African countries. Research shows that 80% of the young people in Nigeria are unemployed, while 69% are job seekers. This was research posted before the outbreak of the pandemic. Since the 'hard-phase' moment felt in the pandemic, there are more unemployed than ever before.

This has majorly (among many other reasons) contributed to a clash between government and the people, to date. Be that as it may, the same young people who have yet to find a solution to unemployment as they increase in number day and night, begin to find an opportunity in negative indulgences such as banditry and robbery, cyber-theft and crime, and many other approaches. These give the country a bad name and add to a decrease in the economy (a downfall).

Most of the countries in the world are now in recession. If an economy is growing, that generally means more wealth and more new jobs. It is measured by looking at the percentage of change in gross domestic product, or the value of goods and services produced; typically over three months or a year.

However, in some ways, some countries were able to mitigate the effect of the pandemic on their citizens and economy.

Economic crises and outbursts can commence in a million ways, however. Regardless of the cause or the manner, it has been confirmed that there is one conventional way to fix it: pump money into the system—a lot of it. This is exactly what America did.

The federal government, under the leadership of Donald Trump, implemented a stimulus package to replace consumer spending power and lessen the heavy economic blow. Since the people were spending less, at the time, the government filled the huge pothole with spending measures which include the CARES Act.

The $2.2 trillion bills were authorized in the early stage of the crisis. Although it was very helpful and lessened the effects of the crisis, it hardly changed the fate of the looming recession.

As the pandemic continues to drag the economy by its hair, the second round of stimulus packages is being looked into, to help salvage the economy's state and prevent a looming recession.

The United Kingdom, on the other hand, adopted the Furlough scheme. Introduced in 2020, the scheme was enacted to prevent employers from laying off their staff, and mitigated an increase in unemployment. At first, the government pays 80% of wages up to a cap of £2,500 per month of people who cannot work due to the pandemic and employees whose employers can no longer afford to pay them.

This system was used throughout 2020, but was later modified in July, 2021. The 80% of the wages now constituted 70% of the government's subsidy up to £2,187.50, and employers were instructed to pay 10% of salaries. This has helped to hold the economy in a stable state while the government encourages employers to hire their employees on a full-time basis, if they are able.

In spite of the negativity(s) which the pandemic has caused in many sectors of the economy; on the other hand, it has helped some other sectors (as well as a number of non-notable skills) burgeon.

Valerie Jarrett said: "We need to be investing in manufacturing and small businesses. We need to be creating a workforce where citizens can compete in a global marketplace because they have the necessary skills. And we need fairness, and we need a sustainable, strong economy that is durable for the future."

A Win-Win for Medicine and Pharmaceutics

The pandemic and lockdown has really proven that the basic keypoint to every nation is the health sector. As Maxime Lagacé has rightly said, "Keep your vitality. A life without health is like a river without water."

Long before the recession, the health sector has always been known for its relevance, in all its ramifications. Thousands of situations have 'come and gone', but the need for medicine holds strong.

Governments around the world have pledged billions of dollars for a Covid-19 vaccine and treatment options. Pfizer has seen its share price fall, but Moderna, Novavax, and AstraZeneca have seen significant rises—a result of the partnership with BioNTech—in regards to the high cost of production and management.

A number of pharmaceutical firms have started distributing vaccine doses, and many countries have commenced their vaccination programmes. Many more, such as Johnson & Johnson and Sanofi/GSK, have joined in vaccine distribution, recently.

The health 'sector' profession, however, obviously had no loose 'no matter how little' policy, either before or after the pandemic. Instead, it held more relevance and was the most 'sought after' of all professions. Even at this, there was a lot of detriment, as many doctors died trying to treat the virus-infected. There were ideas of new drugs and vaccines that could help in finding a cure to people's ailments both during and after lockdown as their sales rates doubled, too.

This made the price of medical attendance increase (after the lockdown), as only the rich and 'well-to-do' could have access to good medical care. Here, again, even if the government had been of help to the masses (by slashing bills), the battle it faced (with the economy) as a result of the pandemic made this a 'hard push'.

The request for hand sanitizers (which is also a product of pharmaceutics) became a priority for consumers as fear of contracting the virus escalated during the dark days of March, while neglected lessons we learned when we were little came back into play (i.e. the washing of hands before and after the use of any object or material). Due to an inability for some to get soap and water daily (as a result of the lockdown),, as it was medically advised that sanitizers could be of better help, due to their effectiveness. This too became a 'necessity', and the Purell product was among the most widely recognized brands at the time.

Purell is a producer of hand sanitizers. The product had been in existence for over 70 years (beginning in about 1933), but was never really highly in demand. Of course, how many people would need a hand sanitizer, if the pandemic had not occurred? The fact that Purell helped people, families, churches, and groups of individuals stay safe no doubt added to the brand's emotional connection with their customers.

Natarelli put the demand in context: "Purell came in Number 2 for increased usage during (COVID-19)." He further said, "The need and desire for Purell and other hand sanitizers reached a boiling point for many when they were sold out everywhere. These products were hoarded and in high demand. Fifty-eight percent of users said they used Purell daily."

Purell, as a case study, also proves how in-demand pharmaceutical products had become; most especially during the pandemic. The industry responsible for the production of Purell is Gojo industries, a company that keeps its financial result private.

However, those in the medical industry (doctors, nurses, pharmacists, physiotherapists, and the likes) also benefitted as their income increased, based on the public demand for medical helps and attention (more than it was before the pandemic breakout) up to the present.

The Aftermath

With all that we went through, it is obvious that the world's economy has already been left in shambles. The pandemic forced everyone across the globe to switch their plans. All fashion, sports, entertainment, and technology events were first canceled, and then modified.

While the monetary impact has not been fully ascertained, it is likely to be in the billions, and is increasing. The pandemic has led to an economic recession that is happening everywhere. The damage is quite evident, and embodies the largest economic shock the world has witnessed in decades.

The punches of a high unemployment rate and that there could be no physical gatherings for workers, shareholders, and others left many people hunkering down at home, with extra time on their hands.

What, then, could one do with all the additional hours? Would they sleep and feed alone, all the while? Definitely, that would be impossible.

As a result of this, many businesses which had existed before the lockdown and, yet, were unrecognized (because of their services and deals, which requires the 'airtime', or the internet) went uphill. Examples of these internet and networking products are the Netflix and Zoom apps. These really raked in profits because they were highly used during the lockdown, as they were the only means by which people could be entertained and could connect for official and family meetings, respectively.

Netflix

In a throwback to these times, many families gathered around and watched their televisions as Netflix became the viewing choice of most customers.

Netflix is a brand that Natarelli and MBLM are familiar with, as it makes the Top 10 list. Natarelli said, "Already a strong intimate brand prior to (COVID-19), consumers use the Netflix brand more during the pandemic." He further said, "With increased time at home and a need to escape, streaming entertainment brands became a desired distraction. Fifty-six percent of customers said they use the brand daily."

It is a reality that the extent to which the brand was streamed by people during the lockdown is of 'no count'. However, since it got well known during the pandemic, it remained the best choice for many, after the lockdown. Many people prefer to watch movies from Netflix rather than search for their desired movies on YouTube and other streaming apps, as it has lots of movies available (including the most recent and older films).

All that love, transferred to Netflix, translated into robust financial results for the tech giant. According to research, Netflix reported second-quarter revenue of $6.1 billion; up 25% year on year, while earnings per share of $1.59 jumped 165%, enjoying a growth of 27% more subscribers during the lockdown period. The company also generated positive cash flow for the second consecutive quarter, which had not been achieved in years. The biggest news is that Netflix added 25.9 million subscribers during the first six months of 2020 – and is still increasing.

The serial shows that Netflix produces are being viewed and streamed all over the world, as they now have viewers who await every new release. All of these 'raked-in profits' were made during the pandemic period. For a product like Netflix, there is thanks for the lockdown.

Zoom

Just as Netflix has grown during the pandemic, the Zoom app also has burgeoned. Given the social distancing and the big move to remote work that transpired in the early days of the pandemic as a result of the strict lockdown, it is easy to see why Zoom would experience the biggest adoption among companies mentioned in this study.

Since there could be no one-on-one conversations, as it was strictly advised to maintain social distance between people, Zoom's easy-to-use, industry-leading, high-class video solutions became the next choice, just so users could catch up (at least, to some desirable extent) with every official meeting. It is not like there are no other means to do this on the internet, but Zoom's ability to include 'more than many' attendees (among some other reasons) make it recommendable above others.

Late last year, Zoom was named a "leader" in the 2019 "Magic Quadrant for Meeting Solutions." That marked the fifth time that Zoom made the list, and its fourth consecutive time as a leader.

Again, just as he had spoken about Netflix, Mario Natarelli, who is a managing partner at MBLM, said, "Not surprisingly, Zoom has become part of our lexicon, like [Alphabet's] Google. He further said, "It uses are broad and varied, from virtual weddings to court proceedings. Fifty-two percent of Zoom customers surveyed said they had been using the brand for a year or less, suggesting they got acquainted with the brand during the COVID-19 pandemic."

Just as illustrations were made about how Netflix has massively burgeoned, Zoom also has a whole lot of 'growing' records attached to its name. Research also clarifies that consumers' wholesale adoption of Zoom translated into blockbuster results for the company. Also, second-quarter revenues of $664 million soared 355% a year, while diluted earnings per share of $0.63 showed that customer metrics were equally robust.

Furthermore, the number of customers with more than 10 employees grew over 370,000, up 458% for the year, while those contributing more than 100,000 in trailing 12-month revenues climbed to 988—a 112% increase.

In addition, the net dollar expansion rate, which measures increased spending by existing customers, topped 130% for the ninth consecutive quarter.

As a result, by empowering both businesses and families to meet digitally, Zoom made the pandemic just a little more bearable. That has driven its stock price up nearly 600% (so far) this year. It has also raked in much profit.

Big business owners now rarely have physical meetings. Instead, they see virtual meetings as the best way to make meetings possible, even if they are not within or around the geographical location in which the meeting is to be held. Hence, the use of Zoom is the most popular of all virtual meeting programs.

A study about consumer brands and the emotional connections they make with the public has identified three brands (Zoom Video Communications (NASDAQ:ZM); Purell (part of privately-held Gojo Industries); and Netflix (NASDAQ: NFLX)) that saw the biggest increase in usage during the COVID-19 pandemic lockdown period, while Zoom and Netflix remain strong after the lockdown, today.

Boom in the PPEs

The outbreak of the pandemic led to the boom of personal protective equipment (PPE) caused by rising demand, hoarding by retailers, panic buying, and misuse.

It soon became a case of high demand without a corresponding supply, making it only accessible to the highest bidder. Healthcare workers rely on PPEs to protect themselves and their patients from infecting others and being infected.

But, the shortage left doctors, nurses, and every frontline worker ill-equipped to care for COVID-19 patients due to limited access to supplies such as gloves, goggles, face shields, surgical masks, and aprons.

Since these are very important items for the times we are in, the prices have skyrocketed due to the surge in demand. Surgical masks have seen a five-fold increase, and respirators and gowns price have doubled. This is a win-win for medicine and pharmaceutics.

***

As much as COVID-19 has destroyed a lot of sectors in the economical arena, it has also made 'green' some other sectors, which has brought about some benefits in and from the tech world. This, we can call 'the economical evolution', which will not yet be stabilized for a few years to come (2025, some researchers predict).

Chapter Six

THE NEW NORMAL

"We humans are resilient. We can learn to thrive in our new normal if we have the mindset and the resources we need to adapt-" Lisa E. Betz

In the words of Greek philosopher Heraclitus, "Change is the only constant in life." The world we live in is ever-evolving and ever-changing, as it is influenced by forces political, social, environmental, industrial, and economic. And at the epicenter of these changes is humanity.

But, it is important to note and understand that we humans are naturally resistant to change. Neuroscience and psychology have discovered that a part of our brains, the amygdala, sees change as a threat, thereby creating an inherent resistance to it. This is especially so if the change comes suddenly and with a life-changing impact, as did those brought about by the coronavirus pandemic.

Before the coronavirus pandemic and subsequent lockdown and isolation, the world we knew was expressive, filled with hugs, kisses, touches of reassurance, and a certain amount of stability and predictability...but the coronavirus pandemic has changed the world as we know it, posing a great problem to humanity.

As the ravages of the pandemic in the global arena are seemingly receding and the lockdowns and quarantine are slowly being eased, we seemed to have stepped out of our homes into a whole new world that plays on an entirely different set of rules. The after-effects of the coronavirus pandemic is far-reaching, and it is evident that some of the changes that came with it have fully come to stay, leading to a 'new normal.'

With the erosion of the status quo and introduction of the 'new normal', the questions that then arise are: how easy is adapting to these changes going to be? How normal is the new normal? How does one adapt to this new normal?

The 'new normal' is not a new conception of the global space. It embodies the striking economic and social transformations that bring about widespread uncertainty and social instability, affecting general lifestyles and perceptions. The term has appeared during the industrial revolution of 1769 to 1840, where abrupt radical changes were brought to human existence; and reappeared during the financial crunch of 2008, which was debilitating in its might. But, the greatest difference between then and now is the deconstruction of physical and social interactions, and the technological drive of this 'new normal.'

The new normal poses a wide range of problems ranging from uncertainty, loss of self, fear, workplace/managerial crisis, and more; and these problems are projected to last for a long time. It is pertinent to understand that the new normal has come to stay, and so we need to learn to adapt to and rise above it, to be able to live a fulfilling life devoid of depression and mental health issues.

A World of Masked Faces

In this current milieu, wearing face masks as a form of prevention against coronavirus has become the norm. It has grown to the extent that entrance into both public and private spaces can be limited if one is without a face mask or evidence of vaccination, making face masks an absolute necessity for being able to carry out daily activities.

It is an incontestable fact that face masks have had a positive influence in preventing and containing the rapid spread of the virus. They have also contributed greatly to easing the strict isolation and lockdown protocols so our daily actives can resume; but in another vein, they are a major factor contributing to the wearing down of the fabric of social interactions and social interconnectedness.

By screening off our faces, face masks obstruct facial recognition, non-verbal communication, and emotional signals between people, creating an internal existential crisis and loss. In markets, schools, stores, eateries, and workplaces, everyone is putting on masks and hiding their faces. This, in itself, forms a basis of fear, mistrust, and uncertainty in a world that is already riddled with a lot of concerns about insecurity, deception, and social ills.

Imagine coming back from work late in the evening, or going out, and someone is seemingly following you from behind with a mask covering their face. You find yourself unable to comprehend the emotions running through the face of the person to be able to determine their intent, raising your internal alarms.

But, you cannot write off the need to wear face masks because of these reasons, or put yourself and others at risk. You need to understand that the use of face masks will remain for a long time, until everyone is fully vaccinated and coronavirus becomes nonexistent. It is a battle between either letting people act freely and letting the virus claim lives, or making little sacrifices, at our inconvenience, to save the whole world.

It is advisable to explore means of communication that will enable you to express yourself verbally and be well understood. Don't be too quick to make judgments on peoples' comments or actions in cases where you can't determine their intent because you can't see their facial expressions, but try to first understand the emotions behind them, before reacting.

Social Distancing

The social distancing that came as a result of the coronavirus pandemic brought with it a whole lot of other negatives, including the wearing down of the fabric of social interactions, and disassociation from society. Some scientists chose, instead, to call it 'physical distancing', advocating the idea that the mere separation from one another of a space of six meters can prevent and break the transmission of the virus. But that does not limit the fact that hugs, handshakes, and close interactions that embody human social life have all been put on hold.

Gatherings are limited to a certain number of participants in communities, people have become wary of each other, and anyone sneezing or coughing in a public place is looked upon suspiciously.

This era of social/physical distancing is fast becoming our reality. Gradually, hugs, handshakes, and other forms of physical expressions of our feelings towards friends and strangers are becoming an abomination. This might carry on for a very long time, looking at the new cases of resurgence of the virus in various locations all across the world.

In the words of Nicholas Christakis, "The coronavirus spreading around the world is calling on us to suppress our profoundly human and evolutionarily hard-wired impulses for connection: seeing our friends, getting together in groups, or touching each other."

Even as social distancing has become the new normal, you should understand that this is just a phase, and it too will pass. Explore verbal mediums of expressing your feelings instead of through touch and face-to-face interactions, and connect with the outside world on social media through the various platforms now available. Video calls, voice calls, and messaging apps will come in handy for keeping human interactions going, and although they don't fill the vacuum left by the absence of physical interactions, to a very large extent, they help reduce the feelings of loneliness and depression that come with social distancing.

Virtual/Remote Workplaces

Amongst other facets of human activities destabilized by the coronavirus pandemic were the economy and the workplace (which witnessed millions of people losing their jobs) and the idea of an ideal workplace. The pandemic and isolation disrupted work processes as we know it, leading to a shift of paradigm from an organizational structure of a group of workers working together within a company building to workers working separately from the comfort of their homes.

This put a big sting on the projections and future-proofing predictions made by organizations and managers about the future of the workplace, with the virtual workplace taking over as the true future of the job. With the advent of quarantine and isolation, work settings moved from physical to virtual and from office to remote, with people working from the comfort of their homes and connecting over the internet.

Tools like Zoom, Skype, and Microsoft Teams have become handy for keeping the workplace moving, and it is evident that, for all intents and purposes, this form of work process has come to stay. Just look at the success it has had in cutting down company expenses on travel to physical meetings, promoting flexible working patterns, creating a quick and seamless connectivity with a wide range of staff, and ease of work.

In the future, a hybrid model of work will probably be developed, with a few working from the office while many work from home, reporting into the office space only on selected days so that the efficiency of remote working can be combined with the social interaction, creativity, and innovativeness that working as a team also brings.

The process of transitioning into a virtual workplace can be tiring and frustrating; especially for people who are not tech-savvy, and, predictably, the ability to use digital skills will soon rank amongst the highest prerequisite to work in any organization. It is therefore important to learn how to navigate the digital tools that allow for virtual connectivity, to be able to stand above the situation and not be caught unawares.

Get experts to educate you on the new digital tools that can aid your work process and seamless delivery of results, and follow up on the new trends in technological advancements to see how they can be useful to you. When work finally moves to the virtual space, you will find yourself able to transition easily with little or no stress, and can even come to enjoy the process, rather than be frustrated due to a lack of technical know-how. Get these skills *now*.

It is also important to make arrangements for your remote working process and conditions. Working from home comes with a whole lot of other physical and emotional challenges; especially if you have kids or stay with family, which can be very distracting. It would be pertinent to carve out your workspace now (which can be a corner in your study or even your room), and obtain the necessary equipment like a table, chair, scanner, or other things that will be needed for your job.

Because the virtual/remote workplace is a digital concept housed on the internet, you would do well to gain basic skills on cyber-security and how to protect company information from falling into the hands of mischievous individuals. Although organizations will also put in place various safeguards to protect the process of their virtual workplace, it is necessary for you to also take personal precautions.

Crosscheck every email, directive, and message from the office until you are sure of its validity, before you proceed, and don't be too quick to click on or follow any link that you are unsure of, especially those which require your personal information and password.

The New Phase of Education and Learning

Isolation and quarantine brought a new face to education, as over a billion students all over the world were sequestered in their homes due to the closure of schools, posing a problem of watching the younger generation and student population spend their time doing nothing and being at risk of regression in their academia for however long the school closure and pandemic lasts. The immediate responses were E-learning (which had been slowly gaining ground before school closures were enforced) and parents home schooling their children, in other cases.

But, this form of learning came with a lot of problems for students, including learning passively; the inability of teachers and parents to fully impart emotions and explore all methods necessary to aid in teaching and understanding for students; changes in student admission processes; and more.

As schools are being opened and studies resume, the new phase of education is a blended process of physical and e-learning, with a lot of focus and premium value given to e-learning, unlike before.

In some climes before this time, degrees and certifications obtained through online schooling held little relevance compared to those gained from attending a physical educational construct, but now that is fast losing meaning as e-learning has become more accepted globally. Materials and degrees from reputable institutions now exist online, affording people from anywhere in the world the ability to study remotely and earn a degree.

Several institutions also allow for a self-paced learning process whereby individuals can go through the process of obtaining a degree at their own pace even if they are working, busy with other projects, or even in jail.

You can choose to explore these options that are now available and key into them to achieve your dream of obtaining an extra degree as you work or carry on with your daily life, getting certifications that will give you an edge in the workplace and sharpen your skills.

A Feeling of Global Togetherness

Social media contributed a lot to get people connected, and aided global interactions during the pandemic even as everyone was sequestered within their homes. Apps like Tik-Tok, Instagram, Facebook, and Twitter provided timely relief for people, serving as sources of entertainment, for the dissemination of information, and reducing the brunt of loneliness and depression.

Through the use of live videos and podcasting available on these various apps, people were able to connect to their favorites all over the world, and also made friends from other places.

Aside from all that, there was also the feeling of togetherness and a united sense of purpose that came with the knowledge that we are all together in the fight against coronavirus, and this went a long way in building a bond of unity. People who had contributed both in cash and kindness to the less privileged around them, and even countries and institutional bodies, were not left out.

In the words of António Guterres, Secretary-General of the United Nations: "A pandemic drives home the essential interconnectedness of our human family…We are in this together – and we will get through this, together."

This goes to show that, deep down, we all care about each other and can come to live together in peace and unity, under the right conditions.

A World of Robots and AIs

In the words of Joel Blit, "The artificial intelligence and robotics revolution that we have been expecting is now at our doorstep…"

The pandemic and its resultant effect of destabilization brought to the forefront a major problem in the labor force. The inability of many to go to work adversely affected the economic and agricultural sectors to the extent that if the pandemic lockdown had continued for a longer period, we might have had another famine.

This has led to an increase in the study and exploration of robotics and AI technologies to mitigate against future reoccurrence, but this also poses an existential problem for the future of labor and work. Many would likely lose their jobs as robots and artificial intelligence are introduced into the workplace, creating yet another crisis.

It is important to become informed about changes brought about due to the creation of new robotic and artificial intelligence technologies, to learn new skills as the new era demands, and position yourself to be amongst the few who will rise above this brewing crisis.

***

The 'new normal' has come to stay, and it is very important to learn, understand, and adapt to the changes it brings with it. 'Restrategizing' and 'Retraining' is a critical process that everyone needs to undergo at this stage, in light of the rapid changes happening in all areas of our daily lives.

This is key to living a life of fulfillment and retaining relevance in one's workplace, family, career, and society.

BIO

Ibrahim is a poet and creative writer. He is a graduate of International Business Management and works as a cyber-security consultant. He hails from Lagos, Nigeria, and believes in the power of words and their impact. When he's not writing, you can find him watching football and listening to music.

AUTHOR'S NOTE

Thank you for the time you have taken to read this book. I hope you enjoyed reading it.

If you loved the book and have a minute to spare, I would appreciate a short review on the page or site where you bought it. I greatly appreciate your help in promoting my work. Reviews from readers like you make a huge difference in helping new readers choose a book.

Thank you!

Ibrahim Olawale

www.ingramcontent.com/pod-product-compliance
Lightning Source LLC
Chambersburg PA
CBHW021446080526
44588CB00009B/716